Love Letters

A collection of poetry, Volume II

By Ayoka B.

AYOKA

Joyinhome Publishing

Love LETTERS

Ayoka B.

Published by Joyinhome Publishing

ISBN: 979-8-9897325-3-1

Love is and always will be a burning topic. There are an infinite amount of artistic expressions of love and there are many types of love. Familial love, erotic love, parental love, platonic love, romantic love, self-love.... Love can be fulfilling, unhealthy, abusive, unconditional, unrequited, obsessive, eternal or undeserving.

The title is a play on words.

The first meaning is literal; what is more romantic than a love letter? In a time of technology when people no longer write letters especially not longhand, pen to paper, this is a lost art. Love letters were an expression of feelings and the writer often created poetry about the object of their desire.

The second meaning explores the very basic element of poetry and language. Letters of the alphabet make up the words to create poetry. A poet or writer is a master of words. A master can evoke strong emotion from simply combining letters in a meaningful way.

I want to capture the different faces of love and share the impact that love has had on my life. Perhaps someone will gain insight into their own. That is my hope.

Diallo

To my child, born from kings
My heart grew wings
When I knew you had come to be.

Doctors said not to hope.
But you had a formidable spirit
From the start,
And I knew in my heart
That God sent you to me.

And I named you Ajani.
Because he who wins the struggle
Will always wins the fight.

When you entered this world
Crystal said that you were "kissed by the ancestors."
And you cleaved to me
Completing my humble family.

Elegant fingers
And a shock of wild curls
Gave character to your tiny being.

Diallo…Be Bold.

*Stretch Mark*s

My skin.
The skin I'm in,
Has **stretched** over the years.
My hips and thighs have patterns
And textures
Of silvery rays when it grew
And became taut
To protect a growing life.
There are sound waves
Punctuating my navel
From when my amazing womb
Cradled precious babies.
We hide
And rub potions and lotions
To make them fade
These badges of Motherhood.

Ode to Woman

Woman,
You are powerful beyond measure.
Those curves, bee sting breasts
Your wild hair and crooked smile...
Whatever "imperfection" you may scrutinize
Know that God carved it for you.

Your intellect, grace
And innate wisdom make you distinctive.
A woman's light is stunning
And precious.
Protect it because thieves understand it's worth.

Each time you feel your heart might tear at the seam
Remember that you are
Perfect.
Penis envy... let's talk about womb envy-
You possess the power to bring forth life,
To mold and nurture it.
You only have to own the power that is within
And wield it for the life that you deserve.

The Green Towel

My Mother doesn't know.
When I was about 8 or 9
I used to drape a light green towel
Over my head.
The edge laid along my hairline
And it would hang down the sides of my head
Giving me length.
I would flip that "hair" back
While I gazed at my reflection.
I danced around our apartment.
I didn't know that I felt unpretty;
Ignorant that the whiteness surrounding me
Made me feel lesser.
My dark, curly hair that flowed down my back
Was covered
By a green towel.

Honeysuckle Air

Caught me some honeysuckle air today.
Just a whiff,
Unexpected…
While driving on the freeway
Windows down, hair blowin', music blarin'
Trying to be carefree.

The sweet, heavy scent reminded me of Grandma's
In the summertime.
Of climbing trees,
Playin' kickball
And eating blackberries and sugar 'til we could burst.
Of running fast with the wind on my face and
barrettes stingin' my back
As my plaits slapped.
That honeysuckle air
Punted me back into memories of my pink and white
Huffy
And rollerskatin' on concrete.
Scraped knees and lightning bugs,
Summer vacation, freeze tag
And the days when my universe consisted of home,
Grandma's house and school.

Caught me some honeysuckle air today.

And I could see Grand-dad in the kitchen,
Fussin' over sugar roses and tiers of buttercream and
promises.
Bright, blue days that stretched forever
And never-ending, gut-busting laughter
Between childhood friends.
The smell of the grill, cherry popsicles
And shit-talking
From relatives playin' Spades.
Sittin' in the cherry tree with Metri,
Gigglin' and talkin', ignorant of the world.
Firecrackers and pop guns
Jumpin' over the pond and catchin' guppies…

That honeysuckle air.

My First Love

Trips to the beach
Weekend shopping sprees
You holding my hand in yours,
Protecting me from the world.
I was your "Boop".
Tall, lean and caramel brown;
A cleft chin and
Beautiful smile.
Your singing drove me to breath-taking giggles-
I thought no one could compare…

My hero
My king
My love.

Lonely days of waiting melted into lonely nights
And inconsolable tears.
Years went by.
You came back, charming as ever.
With your sincere words and tender kisses, that
would lead to

Days unaccounted for

Unexplained.

Broken promises,

Money borrowed.

The shock of your fist knocking me to the floor.

The flashing lights,

Me giving a statement

As a crimson print settled onto my pale cheekbone.

At graduation you came smiling

As if you had a hand in my milestone.

Be nice and smile for the camera, said mom.

You had no right.

My hero

My king

My love.

So save the apologies

And personal attacks on my integrity.

You were an asshole long before the rock

Became your motivation.
I remember Mommy on the floor of my room
With a blood-stained Afro.
Me, wide-eyed in four-year-old feety pajamas
And you, swooping down to take me.

I remember our trip to Florida in a yellow, foreign car
You shimmying up a tree to get me a coconut.
Then twenty years later without decency or restraint,
you shattered that tender memory
with the truth-
A truth that would have changed my identity.

My hero
My king
My love.

So excuse me.

Excuse my contempt.
For you
Your family and
Your life.

Excuse my hardened heart
And inability to trust.
That mean streak that everyone loves to hate-
Lovingly molded by you.

Excuse me,
For shielding my children
From your poisonous nature
And lobotomizing you from my life.

As a woman, my journey continues.
For the one to console me
Who will guide and protect me.
To rub my hair
And tenderly kiss my forehead
As a father would.
To rescue me
From the world
From myself
From you.

A girl never forgets her first love.

Know Thy Self

I have come to find

That a woman who knows herself, can be terrifying

And shake the core of a man.

Now,

This is no condemnation- more of an observation

And my experience

With love.

There have been a few

Whom I blessed with the gift

Of me.

Those whom I wrapped my body and spirit around.

Whose ebony I drank in

Willingly,

Completely

And their soul matched my own.

Then,

That flicker- lightning quick-

That I have come to dread,

Like the sinking feeling of quick sand.

That unspoken goodbye.

An admonishment for stirring your spirit.

I felt your sweet breath

And was the mirror

As I dared you to be

The man that I see,

The man you were born to be.

But again,

Fear was the victor.

He cast Love aside as an unworthy opponent.

That is not to say

That I have never settled for less…

But we are in the here

And now,

You can't give me the one thing that I want.

Ode to the One Who Got Away

A random daydream

And you are transported...

The feel of his breath on the nape of your neck

The melody of her laughter

At an inside joke.

Or the urban campus

Where you met

That creative, bold one.

Do I ever cross his mind,

Fleetingly?

Or am I a footnote

In a forgotten chapter?

Years pass

Then a random occurrence

Sparks an unexpected memory

As vivid as the first time.

A song,

A quirk...

Your pulse quickens and butterflies

Flutter.

Marriage, fatherhood

A fulfilling career

Does not erase that feeling

Which burns just beneath the surface...

Most of us have one,

Or maybe you are

To someone else.

What about the one who got away?

You are my undoing.

I guess I knew it

The second time that I saw you,

The night I thanked God for sending you

Finally.

Sometimes,

I've wished that I could go back to that night,

When your actions mirrored your words.

Before,

You became fond of the stop watch.

And you controlled the timing of our togetherness.

Stop.

Go.

Stop, go.

As if you could stop time

For it silently and endlessly slips by

Mocking us.

Before,

You dipped your paint brush

Into many beautiful, yet undeserving colors

Who did not appreciate your artistry

But provided easy release.

Before,

You broke my heart

And promised yourself to someone else.

Cuz my love is deeper, tighter, sweeter, higher, fire

Didn't you know this

Or didn't you notice?

But love doesn't quit.

It is unconditional

And won't end even when you plead.

So I remain,

Moving forward

Yet rooted in the spot

Where love found me

Because I hid

For so long, until God told me it was safe.

I keep faith for what is in my heart

In the flawed man who is so perfect

To me.

In the unending friendship that I feel

And the private affection that we share.

Because

I want to laugh

Cry

Raise my son

Praise God

Create art

Make love

Build a life

With him.

But first he must reveal himself

And show me that he understands

Love is an action word.

Infidelity

Sentimental gifts,

Lead to

Soft kisses

Exchanged during morning glow

As the mist rises, after a midnight shower in June.

The union of two souls ordained by God is too easily

forgotten.

Inspiration

I found my muse.

She was buried under layers of denial, long hours at work
And not taking time
For me.
Unleashed
Words tumble from my mind and soul-
Words of joy, love, sorrow and hope.
Wanting to be near you, in your space
Breathing the air that you breathe.
No longer willing to fight for control of my emotions,
My thoughts spill across the page,
Singing songs of bliss and freedom.
I want to shout and tell everyone
Yet I want to keep this sweetness to myself
To savor
Alone.

You underestimate the magnitude of my words,
My thoughts,
My passion for you.
They are interwoven with the marrow in my bones
The follicles of my hair

And are a part of me.
My tears, disappointments and orgasms were
preordained
And waiting for your divine entrance.
I crave your taste and embrace
That will again complete me.
Far beyond the physical pleasure that we create
I am spellbound beyond explanation by you.
And yet…
As I write,
I am awestruck
Because we have not even begun
To scratch the surface.

I deserve more,

And so does she

But your energy feels so damn good to me.

Full lips, penetrating eyes

And mischievous wit

Caught me by surprise.

Your devouring gaze betrayed the chivalrous words

Bringing a blush to my cheek

Rarely seen.

Truth be told,

You are slowly creeping into my space

Stirring carnal thoughts that have to be…

Orgasmic.

Don't misunderstand

My yearn is beyond physical,

Your infectious spirit and powerful mind are creating

an indelible mark on my insatiable soul, and-

Am I getting too deep?

Because a sista is wrestling with her moral compass

And I have it pinned to the mat.

Breathe.

I need to clear my head,

My thoughts

And reflect.

Could you be a soul mate

That I found too late?

Deja Vous

It hit me slowly
Like a smile that stubbornly
Opens a face.
Creeping into the synapses of my brain,
The pores of my skin
The sinews of my muscles…
Memories of you,
Of us,
Together.

My mind nor heart had warned me to make
allowances
For you.
It was not until today, now
A day after
Your caresses and kisses
Both tender and ferocious
Awakened a memory
Lodged in the corner of my battered heart
That I thought had forgotten you.
Be kind.

Again

I want to hear you laugh
Again.
I want to see you dance
Again.
I yearn for your lips to brush my ear and touch on my
skin.
I want the easiness of us...
To be your soft place to land.
The butterflies, anticipation and passion-
I want it all again.
And I want it with you.
Let's find it together
Again.

Ayoka B. explores the themes of Womanhood, identity, love, loss and family through poetry, fiction and nonfiction. Her writing is vulnerable and honest which resonates with readers. Through her unique lens as a Black woman and DC native, Ayoka seeks to share the untold stories of mothers, sisters, daughters, friends and wives. Her goal is to help people gain clarity and insight into their lives.

Ayoka has a professional background in public relations and strategic communications. She received a bachelor's degree in Communications from Temple University in Philadelphia, Pa. and a master's degree in Public Communication from American University in Washington, DC. Ayoka is a mother and lives with her family in Costa Rica.

This is the second poetry collection in a series of four books. Her debut novel, *Love At Second Sight*, published in February 2024.